Unit 4

Let's Team Up

Contents

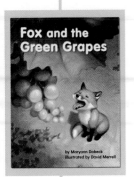

Week 2

Fox and the Green Grapes

long e *(e, ea, ee, ie)*

Fable

Show What You Know

long e *(e, ea, ee, ie)*

-e at the end of long e words

Informational Text

by Meish Goldish
illustrated by Orlando Ramerez

Week 5

Too Much Rain Today

by Doreen Beauregard
illustrated by Nancy Cote

Rain is on Mom's gray rug.
Rain is in Mom's braid.
Rain is on Big Jay's tail.
There is so much water!

I get any pails I can find.
I help Mom.
I catch a lot of rain.

The rain has stopped!
May I run and play?
This yard has
too much mud!

Big Jay can't use
his house.
Big Jay sits and waits.

I see a big rainbow!
It makes us smile.
It's a fine day after all!

Drakes Tail

Drakes Tail Facts

1. Drakes Tail lends the king money.
2. Drakes Tail waits to get paid back.
3. Drakes Tail sets off to get his money.
4. Drakes Tail takes Fox, Pond, and Hive.
5. Drakes Tail gets to be king!

King Facts

1. The king will not pay.
2. The king sticks Drakes Tail in a pen.
3. The king drops Drakes Tail in a big pot.
4. The king is not the nicest king!
5. The king runs away.

My New Words

brain	tail	say	may
play	stray	plainer	plainest
bigger	biggest	grayer	grayest

Fox and the Green Grapes

by Maryann Dobeck
illustrated by David Merrell

Once upon a time,
Fox had a funny dream.
He dreamed of grapes.
Then Fox woke up fast.

"It is late June," said Fox.
"Days are hot and sunny.
The grapes will be ripe.
I know I can find them."

Fox set off across the hill.
"Green grapes are for me,"
said Fox.
"I'll eat all that I see!"

Fox had a nose for grapes.
He saw lots of them.
They sat way up on vines
on tree branches in a field.

Fox went after the grapes.
He ran faster to gain speed.
Then he jumped way up.
But he couldn't reach them.

Fox rose up on his feet.
But it was no use.
He just couldn't reach.

At last Fox gave up.
"This is silly," Fox said.
"I don't want those grapes.
They are not that great."

Gram and James

Gram

Gram helps James ride a bike.

She has a sweet cat named Bean.

Gram teaches James how to make jam.

She likes to read with James.

Gram has fun with James!

17

James

James rides a two-wheel bike.

He likes to pet Gram's cat.

James eats a piece of bread with jam.

James has fun with Gram!

My New Words

me	we	tree	she	sheep
beach	dream	niece	chief	brief
field	leave	please	breeze	sneeze

Grow
and Glow

by Meish Goldish
illustrated by Orlando Ramerez

"This old lot is a mess,"
says Flo. "I wish it were
pretty."

Jo and Mo load trash. Flo holds the bag. Flo's dad Joe mows. The goat mows, too!

Flo says, "Now let's grow." Flo, Jo, and Mo plant seeds all about.

"Please don't grow slow!"
says Flo. "Go, go, go!"
"Give it time," says Dad.

See what has grown. It is
so pretty! Each row glows!

César Chávez

We know him as the man that helped crop pickers. He was known as a wise and bold man, as well. Back then, most crop pickers worked a long day. But they did not get paid much.

25

César told them to go on strike. So the men stopped picking grapes. Then the grapes began to rot. At last, the crop pickers got better pay and homes.

My New Words

no	toast	float	crow	snow
doe	toe	goes	so	roast
belong	between	roadway	loaves	showing

The High Fly

by Meish Goldish
illustrated by Tuko Fujisaki

The bright sun is high in
the sky. My coach yells,
"Try to win! Try, try!"

It's a high fly! I try to find it. The bright sun blinds me.

"Move to the right!"
yells Dwight. "Then you
might see better."

Dwight is right. The light changes. I catch the fly. It's a tie! Fans go wild!

"Thanks, Dwight," I sigh.
"You are kind."
"We are a team," he says.

Frog and Toad Fly a Kite!

What will Frog do?

1. Frog will fly a kite.
2. Frog will not give up.
3. Frog will try and try to fly the kite high in the sky.

What will Toad do?

1. Toad will fly a kite.
2. Toad will run and wave his hands.
3. Toad will jump up and down.
4. Toad will fly the kite high in the sky.

My New Words

my	pie	flies	right
why	tie	tries	kind
spy	wild	cried	myself
light	child	blind	fried

Piggy Is Messy

by Meish Goldish
illustrated by Céline Malépart

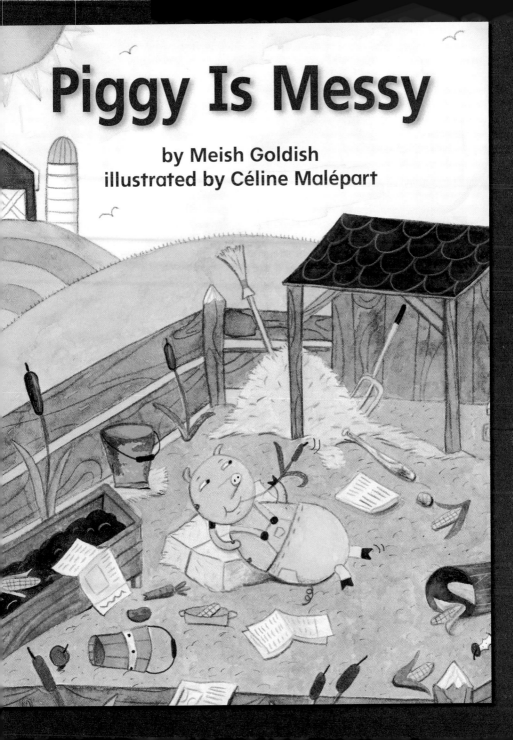

"Piggy!" shout Bunny
and Ducky. "Your home
is so messy and dirty!"

"You should never be so sloppy," says Billy. "We will help you clean."

Bunny finds smelly jelly.
Ducky finds rusty, dusty
cans. They toss them out.

Billy wipes a muddy bat.
He cleans a sticky key.
Piggy is happy. The time
flies by.

"Golly!" shouts Piggy. "Now my home isn't messy. I am lucky! Thank you!"

Animals Team Up

A bird and a giraffe make an odd and funny team. But these pals help each other a lot. The bird eats the bugs on its buddy's skin. That makes them both happy.

The goby fish and the blind shrimp are quite chummy. If danger is close by, the fish flicks its tail. Then the shrimp lets the fish use its hiding place. Having a buddy is the key to staying safe.

My New Words

shaggy	sunny	chilly	penny
alley	valley	hockey	quickly
studied	sandy	babies	ugly
sleepy	money	honey	key

Unit 4: Let's Team Up

to use with *Drakes Tail* **WORD COUNT: 79**

DECODABLE WORDS

Target Phonics Elements

long *a (ai)*
braid, pails, rain, tail, waits

long *a (ay)*
day, gray, Jay, Jay's, may, play

Words Using Previously Taught Skills
a, and, Big, big, can, can't, catch, fine, get, has, help, his, I, in, is, it, it's, lot, makes, Mom, Mom's, much, mud, on, rug, run, sits, smile, stopped, this, us, use

HIGH-FREQUENCY WORDS
Review: after, all, any, find, of, see, the, today, too, water

STORY WORDS
house, rainbow, yard

SHOW WHAT YOU KNOW: Drakes Tail

DECODABLE WORDS

Target Phonics Elements

long *a (ai, ay)*

inflectional endings er, -est
away, bigger, biggest, brain, grayer, grayest, may, nicest, paid, pay, plainer, plainest, play, say, stray, tail, waits

43

to use with *Gram and Me*

WORD COUNT: 137

DECODABLE WORDS

Target Phonics Elements

long *e* (*e*)
be, he, me, the

long *e* (*ea*)
dream(ed), eat, reach

long *e* (*ee*)
feet, green, see, speed, tree

long *e* (*ie*)
field

Words Using Previously Taught Skills

a, and, at, branches, but, can, days, fast, Fox, gain, gave, grapes, had, hill, his, hot, I, I'll, in, is, it, jumped, June, just, last, late, lots, nose, not, off, on, ran, ripe, rose, sat, set, that, them, then, this, those, time, up, use, vines, way, went, will, woke

HIGH-FREQUENCY WORDS

Review: across, after, all, are, couldn't, find, for, funny, no, of, once, said, saw, they, to, upon, want, was

STORY WORDS

don't, faster, great, know, silly, sunny

SHOW WHAT YOU KNOW: Gram and James

DECODABLE WORDS

Target Phonics Elements

long *e* (*e, ea, ee, ie*)
-e at the end of long e words

beach, Bean, breeze, brief, chief, dream, eats, field, he, leave, me, niece, piece, please, read, she, sheep, sneeze, sweet, teaches, tree, we, wheel

to use with *César Chávez* **WORD COUNT: 67**

DECODABLE WORDS

Target Phonics Elements

long *o (o)*
> don't, Flo, Flo's, go, holds, Jo, Mo, old, so

long *o (oa)*
> goat, load

long *o (ow)*
> glow(s), grow, grown, mows, row, slow

long *o (oe)*
> Joe

Words Using Previously Taught Skills
> a, and, bag, dad, Dad, each, has, I, is, it, let's, lot, mess, plant, please, see, seeds, the, this, time, trash, wish

HIGH-FREQUENCY WORDS
> **Review:** about, all, give, now, pretty, says, too, were, what

SHOW WHAT YOU KNOW: César Chávez

DECODABLE WORDS

Target Phonics Elements

long *o (o, oa, ow, oe)*
two-syllable words
> began, belong, better, between, bold, crow, doe, float, go, goes, homes, know, known, loaves, most, no, pickers, picking, roadway, roast, showing, snow, so, toast, toe, told

to use with *The Kite*

WORD COUNT: 70

DECODABLE WORDS

Target Phonics Elements

> long *i (i)*
>> blinds, find, I, kind, wild
>
> long *i (igh)*
>> bright, Dwight, high, light, might, right, sigh
>
> long *i (y)*
>> fly, my, sky, try
>
> long *i (ie)*
>> tie

Words Using Previously Taught Skills

> a, catch, changes, coach, fans, go, he, in, is, it, it's, me, see, sun, team, thanks, the, then, we, win, yells

HIGH-FREQUENCY WORDS

> **Review:** are, better, move, says, to, you

SHOW WHAT YOU KNOW: Frog and Toad Fly a Kite!

DECODABLE WORDS

Target Phonics Elements

> long *i (i, igh, y, ie)*
>
> **two-syllable words**
>> blind, child, cried, fly, flies, fried, high, kind, light, my, myself, pie, right, sky, spy, tie, tries, try, why, wild

to use with *Animal Teams* **WORD COUNT: 68**

DECODABLE WORDS

Target Phonics Elements

long *e (y)*

Billy, Bunny, Ducky, dusty, golly, happy, jelly, lucky, messy, muddy, Piggy, rusty, sloppy, smelly, sticky

long *e (ey)*

key

Words Using Previously Taught Skills

a, am, and, bat, be, by, cans, clean(s), finds, flies, he, help, home, I, is, isn't, my, so, thank, them, time, toss, we, will, wipes

HIGH-FREQUENCY WORDS

Review: never, now, out, says, should, shout(s), they, you, your

STORY WORD

dirty

SHOW WHAT YOU KNOW: Animals Team Up

DECODABLE WORDS

Target Phonics Elements

long *e (y, ey)*

inflectional ending ed **(change y to i verbs)**

alley, babies, buddy('s), chilly, chummy, funny, goby, happy, hockey, honey, key, money, penny, quickly, sandy, shaggy, sleepy, studied, sunny, ugly, valley

HIGH-FREQUENCY WORDS TAUGHT TO DATE

Grade K	Grade I			
a	about	girl	pull	who
and	across	give	put	why
are	after	good	ride	work
can	again	head	run	write
do	all	help	saw	your
for	also	her	says	
go	any	how	school	
has	away	into	should	
have	ball	it	shout	
he	be	jump	show	
here	because	live	so	
I	better	make	some	
is	blue	many	soon	
like	boy	more	then	
little	buy	move	there	
look	by	never	they	
me	call	new	three	
my	carry	no	today	
play	change	not	together	
said	come	now	too	
see	could	of	two	
she	done	old	under	
the	does	once	until	
this	down	one	up	
to	eat	or	upon	
was	eight	other	use	
we	every	our	very	
what	find	out	walked	
where	friends	over	want	
with	from	people	water	
you	funny	place	way	
		pretty	were	

48

DECODING SKILLS TAUGHT TO DATE

CVC letter patterns; short *a*; consonants *b, c, ck, f, g, h, k, l, m, n, p, r, s, t, v*; inflectional ending *-s* (plurals, verbs); short *i*; consonants *d, j, qu, w, x, y, z*; double final consonants; *l* blends; possessives with *'s*; end blends; short *o*; inflectional ending *-ed*; short *e*; contractions with *n't*; *s* blends; *r* blends; inflectional ending *-ing*; short *u*; contractions with *'s*; digraphs *sh, th, ng*; compound words; long *a (a_e)*, inflectional ending *-ed* (drop final *e*); long *i (i_e)*; soft *c, g, -dge*; digraphs *ch, -tch, wh-, ph*; inflectional ending *-es* (no change to base word); long *e (e_e)*, long *o (o_e)*, long *u (u_e)*; silent letters *gn, kn, wr*; 3-letter blends *scr-, spl-, spr-, str-*; inflectional endings *-ed, -ing*; long *a (ai, ay)*; inflectional endings *-er, -est*; long *e (e, ea, ee, ie)*; *e* at the end of long *e* words; long *o (o, oa, oe, ow)*; 2-syllable words; long *i (i, ie, igh, y)*; 2-syllable inflectional endings (changing *-y* to *ie*); long *e (ey, y)*; inflectional ending *-ed* (verbs; change *y* to *i*)

I Have a Friend

BY TIM JOHNSON
ILLUSTRATED BY MARC MONGEAU

Harcourt

Orlando   Boston   Dallas   Chicago   San Diego

www.harcourtschool.com

I have yellow.

I have brown.

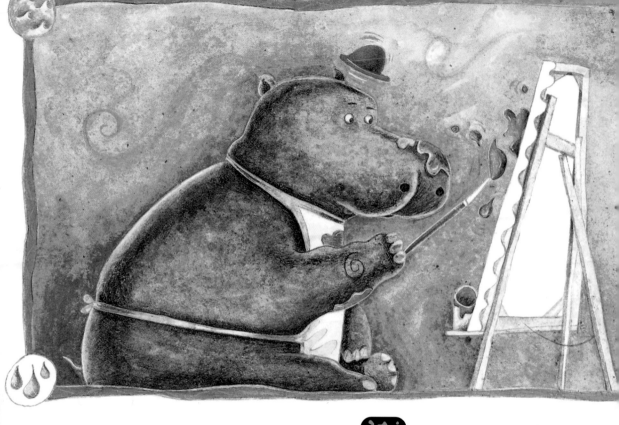

I have blue.

I have green.

I have orange.

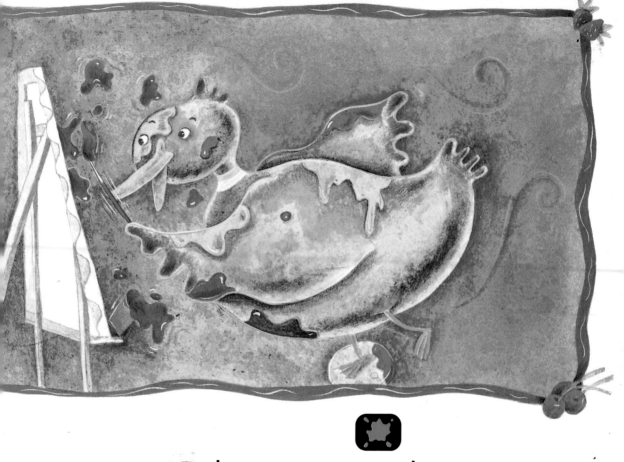

I have red.

I have a friend.